Beautiful

poems by

Eve Forti

Finishing Line Press
Georgetown, Kentucky

Beautiful

ACKNOWLEDGMENTS

I am grateful to the editors who first published these poems sometimes under
different titles and in earlier versions:

Black Buzzard Review: "Who Hasn't Longed To Be?"
Black River Review: "The Garden After Eden"
Common Ground Review: "Beautiful," "If I Were A Spoon"
Off The Coast: "And If Everyone Were...?," "Paris Someday"
Out of the Cradle: "Unexpected Reflections"
RE:AL: "Beethoven's Storm"
San Fernando Poetry Journal: "Connecting Dots"
The Lowell Review: "Can't Wait For Perigee"

"Beautiful" won first prize in the 2013 *Common Ground Review* Poetry Contest

Publisher: Leah Maines

Editor: Christen Kincaid

Cover Art: Liz Forti

Author Photo: Maria Burnham

Cover Design: Eve Forti

Printed in the USA on acid-free paper.
Order online: www.finishinglinepress.com
                  also available on amazon.com

Author inquiries and mail orders:
Finishing Line Press
P. O. Box 1626
Georgetown, Kentucky 40324
U. S. A.

Table of Contents

"Beauty is a short-lived reign."

~Socrates

BEAUTIFUL

She waits out front for him
he said he might drop by
no date
no promise
but she hopes
and wears her new blue sweater set

she knows she is not beautiful
her parents agree

he does not drop by that day
or any other day or night
no date
no promise
after all she is not beautiful

her mirror is a silent witness
to what she has been told

years later when new friends drop by
they see
old photographs of her
and exclaim *how beautiful you were*
she nods
not knowing what to say

PEONIES

I wait all year for them
their sweet perfume
that burst of beauty

then by July they come
crowding all at once
pushing each other aside
falling over
stems unable to hold their weight

a few days of splendor
a few days of unmatched fragrance
and joy

I wait all year
for these unsubtle gems
and then they are gone

ZEN GARDEN

This garden is my garden
a space that I alone have made
by digging and uprooting
not by planting

each day for months
pulling and routing out
weeding and making space
for white butterflies
wind chimes and clay pots
baskets and Buddha
cranes and water fountain
Saint Francis and his birds of cloisonné
small colored stones
large river rocks
and a few semi-precious gems
carefully strewn

rugosa roses still bloom
where I left them
most I pulled out by hand

each day I weed and wait for birds
to come and sing to me
after eating the berries I leave for them

each day I weed and watch the bees
tumble about inside pink petals
rose fragrance filling this garden
that is my garden

ADVISORY

Sometimes in March
wind rages over scrub and pine
across frozen mud and cove

through open fields
littered with branches
twigs and things
we forgot to tie down

sometimes in March
wind roars like a freight
rattling doors
windows and bones

loosening shutters and shingles
small stones on the cairn
bristling

whistling a warning
not to think of spring

BEETHOVEN'S STORM

Squalls of static flooded
his head, blew out his ears.
And he drowned in the quiet
that followed. The hush
of snow falling on water.
The still of snow drifting
on snow. A whiteout of sound.

But the music pursued him
note upon note. Silently
winging like Noah's dove
over the flood. Wooing
his genius-soaked memory
with a promise of symphony.

UNEXPECTED REFLECTIONS

Light bulbs, almost flares,
startle her as she catches
a glimpse in a full-length
mirror in the ladies lounge.

She puzzles whose face,
whose body she sees
and winces, recalling
once searching out mirrors,
seeking lights.

She remembers glossy hair,
unrouged skin, innocent eyes.
Another face, another time.

Now she maintains
it's what's inside that matters.
That wisdom outshines beauty.
And some days she truly believes it.
But never in the blinding light
of unexpected reflections.

SUPERNOVA
Marilyn Monroe 1926-1962

She was a massive star,
but every star is mortal.
The brightest burn fastest,
wildest, hottest, wondrously
more brilliant than the rest.

When her core collapsed
exploding in a burst of light,
for a time she even outshone Venus.

In death her field expanded
with magnetic pull, fierce energy
that still attracts star gazers.
And from her cooling embers
new stars still form.

BEFORE THE READING

The poet sitting in front of me
heard me humming
I told her I can't help myself

I didn't tell her
there is a part of me
that is happy deep down
out of sight and memory

there is a part of me
in the cellar of my heart
that longs to sing

ON THE RIM OF THE SUN

Trillions of galaxies
Each with billions of stars

Across the Milky Way
Through mostly empty space
Our planet wheels with Venus
And the rest around our little blaze

But in a million ways Earth
Is more than size or place
Maybe a million and one
We have saints and poets here
Green flashes on the rim of the Sun
Shimmering   Nonpareil

And even after they are gone
Some of us still sing their songs
And hitchhike on their words
To far places in the cosmos
They can now describe firsthand

Trillions of galaxies
Each with billions of stars

PILGRIMAGE

There are no footprints
in the moat of snow
mostly winged things
seek refuge here tonight

nests of frosted mud
twigs and tinsel specks
perch on granite sills
beneath stained glass saints
who like faded movie stars
have seen brighter days
bigger audiences

flickers of moonlight
on alcoves and statues
on gray marble altars
mimic early silent films

votives no longer flashing
signals in fiery petition
still crackle in dark niches
no censers or smoky perfume
of frankincense and myrrh
no bells

not sure what lures me
even in my sleep
my dreams
              relics of childhood
              remnants of grace
maybe
but birds are here
and they are not questioning
why they fly home

WHO HASN'T LONGED TO BE?

Who hasn't longed to be like Francis?
To speak the language of deer and dog.
To grasp meaning in brays, roars and growls.
To have roses whirl petals, daisies bow,
morning glories burst open in moonlight
because you walk by.
To be called Brother by bluebirds
and robins as they perch on your shoulder.
Who hasn't longed to be special?
To be more.
To be revered by man and beast.
To break all rules, halo intact.

BIRD WATCHING

The same morning
you couldn't wait to tell me
how you unlatched the screen
to help a hummingbird escape
its squeak-cry for help
alerting you to action
I heard a loud thump
against the glass door

a catbird lay dead
next to the red geraniums
on our deck
gray feathers fluffing
ruffling in the early breeze
as if it were trying to fly again

we can't save everything

death nests in our unconscious
takes flight in dreams
waits in the branches of our lives
we close our eyes
hoping to become invisible
in the long shadow of its wings

LILY OF THE VALLEY

Lilies of the valley were in a small glass vase
near the bed
where a little girl was lying as still
as Sleeping Beauty

the mother
bright humming bird
hovered
around her one flower

each time I walked by
she was there

the mother did not want my prayers
she did not need me

I needed her

I needed to know how love
keeps death at bay
transcends reality
stays hopeful
even in the hopeless hours

CONNECTING DOTS

If we saw ourselves
and one another
unchecked by bounds
of human vision,
who could stand the view?
Who would console us?

No skin and bone
or solid flesh,
just atoms circling
in the void.
Unconnected dots.
An intermingling
of ourselves with all
we touch and they with us.

Who could bear the burden
of such oneness,
so much space?
So much me a part of you
and you of me.

How could we linger
in that hollow
between what we are
and what we imagine
ourselves to be?

AND IF EVERYONE WERE...?

If everyone were blind
how would we know who to hate?
Would we choose those
with high-pitched voices
or baritones? Would altos
aggravate us enough to kill?
Could contraltos vote or move
into our neighborhoods?
And how suspicious would we be
of bassos or the tone deaf?
Perhaps our jails would overflow
with tenors or with poor souls
who could not sing at all.

FALLING UP

He lives on the edge
in breathless ways

drives like the wind
in hurricanes

through lightning storms
to the ocean's ledge

sea-slick crags and rocky strand
stands on tip-toe

arms spread wide
a white gull perched for flight

gleaming through
a turbulent darkness

feeding fear
to a hungry sky

THROUGH A CLEAR PANE OF GLASS IN WINTER

New flakes falling
gray Atlantic islands
dotted with pines
frosted with snow

fresh deer tracks
and marks unknown
in yesterday's storm
icicles freezing high
above the window frame

cold wind whistling
fishing boats
far from shore and safety
deep ocean harboring
a promise of things wild

galaxies colliding
big bangs
suns bouncing off suns
flashes of blinding light
and furious beauty

heavenly dreams
knowing where I am
and where I want to be
not knowing how to get
from here to there

CAN'T WAIT FOR PERIGEE

He says the sun's interior temperature
is twenty-nine million degrees Fahrenheit.

She says she feels cold.

He says a storm has been raging on Jupiter
for over three hundred years.

She says she's bored.

He says there are more than a quadrillion
galaxies in the universe.

She says she's lonely.

He says life originated on Earth
over three billion years ago.

She says she feels old.

He says it is twenty-six trillion miles from Earth
to the nearest star outside our solar system.

She says she needs to get away.

He says the starlight of tonight left
the farthest visible galaxy five billion years ago.

She says it's been a long time coming.

He says one million seconds equals eleven days,
one billion seconds equals thirty-two years,
one trillion seconds equals thirty-two thousand years.

She says life's too short.

He says apogee is the point in the orbit of the moon
at the greatest distance from Earth.

She says that's close enough.

A NATURE STORY

Their egos clashed
crashing
in one big bang
folding like rocks
in a continental collision
pleating at silent depths
burning

slow to cool down
they separately reformed
into dry shale barrens
stark and crusty
forever fragile

over the years
they bandaged old wounds
with rue and aloe vera
moss tufts and phlox
forget-me-nots
and mountain clover

a beautiful cover

THE GARDEN AFTER EDEN

On this second wedding night
he doesn't need champagne or cliché.
He's swallowed both before.
Now he needs a lightning bolt,
a jolt to the brain. He needs
to forget, to snuff out memories,
the scorched August of the first time.
Incomparable, at least in retrospect.
Can firsts ever be compared?

Imagine Adam in that first instant
when he felt that he wasn't alone.
When he pressed against her leaf on leaf.
Could anyone ever equal Eve?
Well, who knows the name of the second
woman? The garden after Eden?

A DOG

Sometimes I think about getting a dog

small and compact
a Pug or a Pomeranian
I once had a Pekinese
found at a shelter
she had been abused

it took almost two years
for the pain to leave her eyes
maybe it went to a deeper place inside

I loved her and I think she loved me
or at least she trusted me
and in the long run
perhaps
that is what love really is

Sometimes I think about getting a dog

I'D MOVE IN TODAY IF I COULD

My young grandson colors
with neon markers
a picture of the house he will buy
for us to share
when we return from our trip to the moon

it is a large brick building
overlooking the East River

in one corner is a tiny yellow square
with water view deemed mine

the rest of the building is all his
which he thinks is fair
because he is drawing the picture

IF I WERE A SPOON

I would be a runcible spoon
scooping soft seeds
from a fragrant green melon
or a polished silver spoon
saved for anniversary parties
and other balloon-filled occasions
maybe a dainty demitasse spoon
next to an espresso cup
on a table in a small café
in Paris or Rome

measuring spoons
wooden spoons
ladles
scoops
big dippers
choices galore

if I were a fork I would be a runcible spoon
mincing quince
for homemade preserves
or an elegant sterling pickle fork
reserved for formal luncheons
maybe a giant trident
like the one carried
by Poseidon
in his underworld realm

table forks
salad forks
meat forks
hay forks
pitch forks
choices galore

as it is I am an old knife
stuck in the corner of a kitchen drawer
waiting to be sharpened

THE PARC MONCEAU

Claude Monet, oil on canvas 1878

A hedge of young ladies
trimmed,
waiting for secrets
to drop like pied leaves
onto their whiteness.
Untold.

A hedge of young ladies
sculpted
by an afternoon of dreams,
waiting for someone
or something to happen.
Unpainted.

PARIS SOMEDAY

Promise when we're old
we'll meet in Paris

lounge at sidewalk cafés
sip young wine
toast our longevity

we'll contemplate cuisine
and world affairs

watch the young
gallop to their mistakes

wink at handsome men
and ogle beautiful women
no one will notice or care

we'll stroll boulevards arm in arm
chatting to strangers
waving at taxis
buying useless trinkets
and baskets of musky blossoms

employ no maps or itinerary
no must dos or can't miss

we'll have nothing but the moment
and the mettle to live it

Eve Forti, born in Boston, now lives on the coast of Maine with her husband, Tom. She taught elementary and high school and was a hospital chaplain, a campus minister, and a member of Spiritual Directors International for twenty years. Forti was on the Maine team that competed at the National Slam Poetry Finals in Asheville, North Carolina in 1994.

Her poems have appeared in *Asheville Poetry Review, Atlanta Review, Off the Coast,* and *Common Ground Review* among other publications. She received six International Awards from *Atlanta Review* between 2007 and 2015. Her poem "Beautiful" won first prize in the 2013 *Common Ground Review* poetry contest. Her poem "At The Metropolitan Museum Of Art" was selected to be in the 2016 anthology, *Take Heart, More Poems From Maine.* It first appeared in her chapbook, *Holding My Breath*, published by Finishing Line Press in 2012.